Run a Lap

Written by Natasha Paul

Illustrated by Yoss Sánchez

Collins

bell

lid on a cup

bell

lid on a cup

fan

run o**ff**
· · · · ·

fan

run off

red hat
. . . . . .

big mess

red hat

big mess

🐾 Review: After reading 🐾

Use your assessment from hearing the children read to choose any GPCs and words that need additional practice.

Read 1: Decoding

- Use grapheme cards to make any words you need to practise. Model reading those words, using teacher-led blending.
- Look at the "I spy sounds" pages (14–15) together. Ask the children to point out as many things as they can in the picture that begin with the /l/ sound. (*lunch, lunchbox, lolly, ladybird, lion, lettuce*) Repeat for things that end in "ll". (*doll, shell, ball, bell*)
- Ask the children to follow as you read the whole book, demonstrating fluency and prosody.

Read 2: Vocabulary

- Look back through the book and discuss the pictures. Encourage the children to talk about details that stand out for them. Use a dialogic talk model to expand on their ideas and recast them in full sentences as naturally as possible.
- Work together to expand vocabulary by naming objects in the pictures that children do not know.
- On pages 10 and 11 ask: What word tells us the colour of the hat? (*red*)

Read 3: Comprehension

- Look at the picture on pages 2 and 3. Ask the children to tell you what's going on in the picture. Ask: Have you ever taken part in a race like this? What happened?
- On page 6, ask: What is the teacher doing? (e.g. *waving a fan*) Why do you think she is doing this? (e.g. *she is hot*)
- On pages 10 and 11, ask: What is the **big mess**? (e.g. *a pile of things from the sports day*)